Betrayal of Hope

poems by

Victor Rumanyika

Betrayal of Hope

Victor Rumanyika

ISBN 978-1-8383677-0-1

Published by Victor Rumanyika Publishing in conjunction with Writersworld, this book is produced entirely in the UK, is available to order from most book shops in the United Kingdom, and is globally available via UK-based Internet book retailers.

Cover design by Jag Lall

Image Gerd Altmann, Pixabay
Image, Myriams-Fotos, Pixabay

Copy editor: Sue Croft

WRITERSWORLD

2 Bear Close, Woodstock,

Oxfordshire

OX20 1JX

United Kingdom

www.writersworld.co.uk

The text pages of this book are produced via an independent certification process that ensures the trees from which the paper is produced comes from well managed sources that exclude the risk of using illegally logged timber while leaving options to use post-consumer recycled paper as well.

Dedication

to

Gabriella, Shaun, and Anne, with love

Foreword

These poems are about the betrayed hopes that many have in new leaders who always promise to change things for the better and put the interests of the common person first: but never do.

They bemoan the prevalence of widespread systematic corruption and greed for power.

They address issues such as the failures in the health sector, rampant corruption, and nepotism.

They were written during an election period where many young people stood up and challenged the status quo.

Many of these young people have been imprisoned or murdered by the state, and yet the judiciary and other arms of the state remain powerless to bring order.

They are relevant to any part of the world where these injustices prevail.

CONTENTS

DECEMBER 1969	1
ORDERS FROM ABOVE	2
THE MIRAGE	3
BEFORE 1986	4
BETRAYAL	6
TRAVELLING THROUGH BUDDO	8
"SUBSTANTIAL EFFECT"	9
CISSY	10
EQUALITY	12
EXHIBIT 1505	14
FREEDOM	16
GOD'S CHILDREN	17
HOW MUCH BLOOD is ENOUGH?	18
HYPOCRISY of the BISHOPS	19
REASSURED	20
JE SUIS L'ÉTAT!	22
KATUMBA OYEE!!!	23
KING KONG	24
JANUARY 1986	25
LAWLESSNESS	26
LITTLE SWEETENER	28

LIVING in a GILDED CAGE   30

MAKINDYE   31

MÉNAGE à TROIS   32

THE DOVES THAT REFUSED to FLY AWAY   33

MUSIC is a WEAPON   34

LIARS   36

THE BOAT   38

THE PRINCESS   40

SECURING YOUR FUTURE   42

SCIENTIFIC CAMPAIGNS   43

THE ABYSS   44

THE DRONE   45

THE DREARY SWAMP   46

SPREADING COVID-19   48

COVID BONANZA   49

THE COURT MARTIAL   50

CONFLICTED POLICE   51

GHETTO! CAN ANYTHING GOOD COME FROM THERE?   52

ELECTIONS AND COUPS   53

THE GATHERING   54

PESTILENCE   56

THE MEANDERING BUS   57

THE VOLUNTEER   58

ORGANISING ELECTIONS or COUP?   60

CATFISHING   61

THE BAYAYE   62

HATCHET MAN   63

THE MARKET   64

WE ARE REMOVING a DICTATOR   66

THE FART   68

THE FLAG   69

OOMPA LOOMPA MINISTER   70

THE NEW CONSTITUTION   71

ODE to MUKWANO   72

DISASSOCIATIVE EPISODES   74

SMALL TALK   75

TEAR DROPS   76

POETIC JUSTICE   78

A PYRRHIC VICTORY   79
Election January 2021

DECEMBER 1969

The day that the president
Was discharged from Mulago hospital;
The national referral hospital
After having surgery
Having survived an assassination attempt.
The health system then was efficient.

Forty years later,
The health system is in its death throes.
Abandoned by a regime
That prioritises
The purchase of tear gas.

Corruption and nepotism have taken root.
The oxygen suppliers are his in-laws
And responsible administrator,
His daughter.

The emperor and his family
Do not use the national health facilities,
They are not good enough for them.
And yet, he calls himself a nationalist.

Maybe, we were better off in December 1969.

ORDERS FROM ABOVE

They have been granted bail
And a production warrant issued
For them to be released
From prison.
Soldiers surround the prison,
Preventing their release.

The soldiers do not present
Any authority for their actions,
But state that
They are following
"Orders from above".

The soldiers stop rallies.
The civilians are living in fear.
The courts are fearful.
Musicians are not allowed to perform,
And the custody clock is not observed
On the instructions of
"Orders from above".

THE MIRAGE

Just as it was at the conference
When the land was shared
Amongst themselves, or
In the Congo Free State
That was owned by King Leopold II.

The land is being shared
By a new set that did not come
Clothed as trading companies.

The new set arrived in 1986
As freedom fighters on a mission
To free us.

Led by a charismatic leader,
They sloganeered
'This is not a mere change of guards',
Promising a fundamental change.

The new set lords it over us,
Promising us prosperity for all.
And yet
The leader works for himself and his family.
The promised freedom
Is but a deception by the new set.

BEFORE 1986

We engaged in bulungi bwa'nsi or communal work,
on Saturdays.
The police turned up to crime scenes
In their crisp blue uniforms
And took fingerprint samples.

National immunisation programs
Were carried out in all primary schools.
The health service was efficient and
The hospitals had medicine and doctors.
No one travelled abroad for medical treatment.
The country was not created in 1986

Kayoola trains provided
A regular train service.
There were regular internal flights
To different airports within the country.
The commercial bank
Had branches across the country.
The country was not created in 1986.

Farmers sold coffee
To the coffee marketing board.
We purchased milk
From the dairy cooperation.
The country was not created in 1986.

The city and towns were orderly
And pupils did not have to leave home
At 5 am to avoid the traffic congestion.
We played in the school fields
That have since been sold off.
The National Theatre hosted school music competitions.
The country was not created in 1986.

Corruption was frowned upon.
All the national borders were open.
UTC buses traversed the country.
The cooperative bank provided
Affordable loans to the farmers.
The country was not created in 1986.

They want us to believe
That they created the country in 1986.
But we remember with nostalgia,
The country before 1986.

BETRAYAL

They were your friends
Whom you believed in.
You promoted their cause,
Campaigned for them
Was imprisoned for them and
Voted for them.

But they forgot about you
And everyone else.
Enriched themselves,
Grabbed the economy,
Looted the state coffers,
Rigged the elections and
Rewarded their families.

Now, they oppress us
Change the constitution
Divide us.

When we speak up
They abduct us and
Torture us.

They have destroyed
What they found.
Turned us
Into their slaves, or
Exiled us.

As you are not
With us anymore,
At least
You do not see what they have become.

TRAVELLING THROUGH BUDDO

He takes a detour to avoid the heavy traffic.
Not long ago
This was a remote area
That is now bustling with frenzied activity.

Music blares from the speakers placed on a vehicle.
The small dirt road is congested
With half-dressed children
And ordinary adults going about
Their daily chores.

Life here is a struggle.

"SUBSTANTIAL EFFECT"

"The elections were not free or fair.
There were electoral malpractices
And rigging.
But this did not
Substantially affect
The outcome of the elections.
Therefore, the election results
Have been upheld."

This has been the routine outcome
Of electoral petitions.

They never define what
"Substantial effect" is.
It now sounds like a broken record.
The population, that has always looked on
As these circuses play out,
Is now at the end of their tether.

Next time,
They might not return to these courts
But "substantially affect" the outcome themselves!

CISSY

The manholes leading to the drainage channel
Are missing their covers.
During heavy downpours and flooding
It is not possible to see the gaping holes
As they are right in the middle of the flooded
Public walkways that those that do not drive
Are forced to use.

She is a middle-aged woman
In her late fifties,
Returning home from the market
Where she works as a vendor.
She is walking blissfully
In the falling rain
When she suddenly disappears,
Consumed by one of the gaping holes.

Some men try to help her out,
But the current is too strong,
Overpowering the men and swallowing her
Into the vast channel
That drains the city.

The limp city council
Is responsible for the drainage channels,
But has abdicated its responsibility.
A month later,
Her decomposed remains are recovered,
Far away
In a swamp by the lake
Where she is identified by her clothing.
Her name is Cissy Namukasa.

EQUALITY

All I seek
Is equal treatment.
Not any favours or
Anything that,
I don't deserve.
I desire,
To be treated
Like the next person.

I observe
Their haunted looks,
Blank faces and
Feigned ignorance.
I seek
To be treated
Like the next person.

Not judged
By the size of my bum,
the sharpness of my nose
Or the dark tone of my skin
That have no bearing
On my abilities.

They become
Passive aggressive or
Retreat into
Self-entitled cocoons.
They fake despair
Because I seek
To be treated the same
As the next person.

EXHIBIT 1504

He is one of the untouchables
That has been a perennial official
Involved in corruption and abuse of office,
Yet trusted by the regime.
He is exhibit 1504

He has been involved
In the fraudulent acquisition of government entities.
During the flawed privatisation process
He acquired the lucrative ground-handling services
Of the national airline
After it had been liquidated.
He is exhibit 1504

He is involved in the oil contracts
As a beneficiary of kickbacks.
Named as a mastermind of land-grabbing scams
And owns expensive malls and prime land.
He is exhibit 1504

Regarded as the wealthiest individual,
In the republic.
He has benefited from government contracts
And has monopolies over several imports.
He is exhibit 1504

He is involved in compensation court cases
Where government losses are arranged,
While he schemes off compensation awards.
He is exhibit 1504

He has been named
In the passport for gold scandal
Where foreign officials were issued
With national passports
In exchange for gold bars.

He has been named
In the solicitation of bribes
From the sale of a hotel.
In receiving kickbacks
From the supply of ballot papers.
He is exhibit 1504

His wealth is hidden
In a myriad offshore accounts.
The parliament has censured him for corruption
At the General Assembly;
He solicitated a bribe from a foreign investor
That was convicted of corruption.
Yet, he remains named as exhibit 1504

FREEDOM

They want to lock us away,
Confine us, enslave us,
Rob us
In this place.

They want to
Arrest us, beat us,
Divide us, take our lands
Lakes and rivers,
Rule us,
Turn us into beggars
In this place.

They want to
Stop us from speaking,
Kill us, destroy us,
Follow us,
Spray us with pepper spray
In this place that we call home

They found us
Humble and peaceful,
With traditional values
Of love and respect
That they have eroded
With their crudeness.

Now that we have
Purged fear from our hearts,
We refuse their rule.

GOD'S CHILDREN

How many times shall I call you?
You know what to do
To free yourselves from this prison.

Even if they break our legs
Or make us blind.
How many times shall I call you?
They have done every evil thing.

They have sold us.
Today's youth;
How many times shall I call you?
You know what to do.

God's children,
Even if they threaten us
They are not God.
Don't fear them
God is with us
You know what to do.

HOW MUCH BLOOD is ENOUGH?

For how long are you going to kill your children?
Have you not got any shame?
You have killed for decades.
You are nearly eighty years old
Yet you continue to kill your children.

How much blood is enough
To quench your thirst?
Have not enough died in your senseless wars?
Why do you crave more blood?
For how long are your children
Going to be killed?

Yasin Kawuma was killed on 13 August 2018.
Rita Nabukenya was killed on 24 February 2020.
Dan Kyeyune was shot in the head on 25 February 2020.
54 others were killed on 18 and 19th 2020 during protests.

You gloat at their death
Or offer compensation for their lives
That have been snuffed out.
How much money is a life worth?
For how long are you going to kill your children?

HYPOCRISY of the BISHOPS

Where is your conscience?
That you don't feel the pain of your flock
That are yearning for change.
Your flock,
That are being repressed.
Why are you indifferent to their suffering?

Why have you lost your souls?
Did you not have any?
Are you like Prophet Hananiah?
That persuaded the nation to trust in lies.

When you speak,
Your words sooth the oppressor.
Others before you
Were bold men of God
That listened to the voice of God and
Not to worldly rulers.

Archbishop Luwum paid the ultimate price.
Bishop Kivengere did not bow down to the oppressor.
Yet, you flatter him.

Your people are in iron yokes
Yet you speak with forked tongues.
You know the truth but
Choose myrrh from the oppressor.

REASSURED

By the presence of my parents,
I try not to peek out of the closed windows.
When I do,
I spot flashes of red tracer bullets,
Lighting up the sky like Christmas lights.

In the morning,
Everyone is instructed
To leave.
The area is now part of the frontline.

We seek refuge in a neighbourhood
A few miles away.
Strangers accommodate
And feed us in their homes.
The diet consists of boiled cassava, yams, and beans.

A few days later, the fighting ceases.
Crowds gather
By the main arterial road
Leading to the airport
And watch as victorious rebel soldiers
March towards the city
From the direction of the airport.

Humiliated and defeated,
Government soldiers are marched past the crowds.
Vehicles and trucks,
Loaded with captured weapons and ammunition,
Follow the marching rebels.

We make our way back home.
The area is teeming with rural-looking
Dark, tall rebel soldiers.
Some have curly hair.

They look like,
The herdsmen and local men
That I often see
Selling fermented milk in traditional gourds
By the roadside at Itojo,
On the road to Kabale.

They appear lost and awed.
They are in unfamiliar territory.
Perhaps this is their first time
To come this far
From the cattle-rearing territory.

They are disciplined
And mind their own business.
Several days later, we make our way
To the city centre
Whose streets are littered with,
Swollen and decaying dead bodies.

January 1986,
The year
That a 34-year regime
Came into power.

JE SUIS L'ÉTAT !

The emperor decrees that
The families of the murdered
"Innocent" victims
Will be compensated.
Families of murdered "rioters"
Will not receive any compensation.

His subjects' lives have a price.
The going rate 1500 dollars
For each "life".

We are back to Leopold II
And the Congo free state.
Where a native's worth
Was measured
In terms of rubber collected,
Or ivory provided.

The price for rebelling
Was amputations,
Or lashes
With the dreaded chicotte.
Now, it is 1500 dollars
For a "rioter's" life.

KATUMBA OYEE!!!

At 24 years of age,
John Katumba is the youngest contestant
In the presidential elections.
Considered a clown by some.
A government project by others.
He was nominated by the electoral commission.

He walked to the nomination venue,
When his derelict car
Broke down
And was sent away
To clear the nomination fees.

He has traversed the country
Winning admiration
For his determination and resilience.
Been harassed by the state
But has kept his amiable smile.

Katumba oyee!!! is his slogan
That has captured hearts
Of smitten suitors.
He remains irrepressible.

Katumba oyee!!!

KING KONG

He screams at the camera,
Saliva drooling over his thin lips.
"We shall kill you", he rants,
Exposing a gap in his front teeth.

He insults the opposition leader's wife
As having pointed teeth
Like ensonzi, a type of mud fish.
Wiping the sweat off his face,
He broadcasts with impunity.
The authorities don't tame
His genocidal talk.

He threatens to kill
A pregnant rival's unborn child
By stomping all over the foetus.
The state is mute.
He calls himself King Kong.

He offends Muslims
Yet claims to be one.
"Jalla jalalu", he exhorts
Whilst calling himself
A "European Muslim".

He is a recent returnee
From economic exile
Where he lived
For the last ten years:
But has found favour
With the ruling powers
That had caused his economic exile.

JANUARY 1986

That day, I planned to go and play lawn tennis
At the Club but was stopped
From going there by my parents.
It is not safe, I am told, and
Have to remain at home.

My parents have gone to the city
To work.
But have, like many others,
Returned home in a hurry.

We all gather inside the house
Where the doors are shut.
Ferocious gunshots ring out from afar.
The rebels are closing in
On the city
And engaging the government forces
That are defending the city in mortal combat.

Though only eleven years old,
This is going to be the third military takeover
That I am witnessing in my young life.
Home is in Lower Makindye,
An area sandwiched
Between two major army garrisons
That are the prime targets of the rebel advance.

At night,
The sound of gunfire intensifies
And is drawing ever closer;
Too close for comfort.

LAWLESSNESS

"Wowee, wowee . . ."
screams the lord mayor
As he is brutalised
By mean police officers
Tightly squeezing his genitals
Before bundling him
Into their vehicle.

He is a human rights activist
Having a lunchtime meal
With his colleagues
When he is abducted,
Blindfolded
And whisked away
To one of their dungeons.

The Nakawere, a mother that has
recently given birth,
Together with
Her new born

Are grabbed by shadowy men
From her home
In the middle of the night
And taken
To an unknown place

They claim to be civilised
And respecters
Of the rule of law,
But their actions
Are those of lawless goons
That flout the law
With impunity.

The days ahead are gloomy
As they defile the land.

LITTLE SWEETENER

Driving back to the city
From upcountry
By the main road,
Is a police vehicle on the roadside
With armed officers
Standing next to it.

The driver slows down
But it is too late,
He is flagged down,
Panicking and sweating.
He is asked to produce his permit
Which they quickly seize.

I scan the roadside
And hidden in a trench
Is an officer with a speed gun.
This is ridiculous.

The driver is ordered out
And accused of speeding.
He is trembling
And this emboldens
The officers
Who continue to rebuke him
As he pleads for mercy.

I exit the vehicle
And gently approach the officers,
Who pretend to write out a ticket
For his infringement.

They ask for "something"
And we begrudgingly
Offer a little sweetener.
This is corruption,
I muse,
And shouldn't be part of it.

The predicament is –
Regardless of where the fine is paid,
Someone is going to appropriate it.
They take it and return
The licence to the driver.

With baited breath,
I caution them about
Laying ambushes
With speed guns.
They make small talk about
Community initiatives,
Leaving me amazed
At their sense of irony.

Noticing I am far from impressed
They laugh sardonically.
It is time to proceed.

LIVING in a GILDED CAGE

He threatens the population
From a place of safety,
Surrounded by loyalist soldiers,
He uses Twitter
To convey messages of fear.
He lives in a gilded cage.

He provokes activists
With his tweets.
He conveys political messages,
Yet he is a serving soldier,
Barred by military regulations
From engaging in partisan politics.

He courts controversy
In a way
No serving soldier would.
Because his father
Is the commander in chief.

He lives in a gilded cage.

MAKINDYE

This is where I was raised
During the chaotic eighties
Of civil strife.
Like elsewhere,
Makindye has expanded.
It is breaking at the seams.

Unplanned development flourishes.
Residences and rentals
Are dotted
In every nook and cranny,
In what were farms and gardens.
The previously dusty road,
Has even been tarmacked.

Gone are the dreaded roadblocks,
Replaced by
A hive of nightlife
And beaming music scene.
The conservative community
Replaced by exuberant youth,
Filming music videos
Or glued to their smartphones.
I muse with mixed nostalgia,
About Makindye.

MÉNAGE à TROIS

Jerome was caught pants down
With a wayward lover
That surprised Jerome
With a sharp spear,
Pointed at Jerome's throat.

The wayward lover
Had parted ways
With her jealous partner.
She had sought
Comfort with
The younger Jerome.

Just like the scorned partner,
General Tibu is holding
A pointed spear
To the neck of his Jerome.
His estranged lover
No longer loves General Tibu.

General Tibu holds elections
That he rigs because
His estranged lover
Prefers to be with Jerome.

THE DOVES THAT REFUSED to FLY AWAY

Doves are often released by clergy
As a symbol of peace.
The clergy have been insensitive
And remained quiet
As civilians
Grappled with injustice.

The clergy continued receiving gifts
From the oppressor.
They requested that elections
Are cancelled
And that the oppressor's rule is extended.
Yet, their flock desire change.

They called a meeting
To say prayers for the country
Ahead of the polls.
At the end,
They released the doves.

To their embarrassment,
The doves refused to fly
And remained rooted firmly on the ground.

MUSIC is a WEAPON

They fear his music
Because of its message
So, they ban his music
Because his songs
Expose them.
    They fear his music.

His music contains
Messages of hope and defiance.
He is not allowed to perform
Or sing in their kingdom.
    They fear his music

They control the coercive
Arms of the state
The police, army, and judiciary.
They have tonnes
Of weapons and tear gas
    But they fear his music.

He confronts them
With his music.
When they harass him
He sings to them.
Everyone else loves his music
    But they fear his music.

He has awakened
The sleeping population
That had lost hope.
Everyone listens to his music

But this frightens them.
  They fear his music.

A citizen holds a portable speaker
And approaches a lone soldier
Whilst he dances to his music
That is blasting out of the speaker.
The soldier doesn't know how to respond.
  That is why they fear his music.

His music speaks to the soul,
Touching places
That money cannot reach.
Young and old
Are inspired by his music
  That is why they fear his music.

His music communicates
Ideas that
They want to keep hidden
From the population.
  That is why they fear his music.

The dancing citizen
Picks up his portable speakers,
Shakes the soldier's hand
And walks away.
His music is a stealth weapon
That does not miss its target.
  That is why – they fear his music.

LIARS

They call Idi Amin's regime
A reign of terror.
Yet they illegally hold suspects
That the courts
Have ordered them to release.
They call Idi Amin barbaric,
Yet they break into private homes
In the dead of the night
And abduct civilians.
They are liars.

The say Idi Amin was cruel,
Yet they place detainees
Under their seats on their patrol vehicles.
They are liars.

They call Idi Amin a tyrant,
Yet they stop
Opposition candidates from campaigning.
They tear-gas civilians
And brazenly rig elections.
At least, Idi Amin did away with the pretence.

They call Idi Amin a buffoon,
Yet they hold suspects in ungazetted places
That they call safe houses.
They intimidate the courts
And render them impotent.
They are liars.

They call Idi Amin a murderer,
Yet they kill their opponents
By faking accidents,
Poisoning them,
Or shooting them.
They are liars.

They call Idi Amin corrupt,
Yet they own all the prime properties,
Own the lakes,
Factories, schools, and hotels.
"Corrupt" Idi Amin did not own any properties.
They are liars.

They call Idi Amin a xenophobe,
Yet they have expelled their own citizens
From their ancestral land,
Exiled many
And sold others into slavery
To work as domestic servants
In the middle east.
They are liars.

They have no moral authority
To call Idi Amin anything.
Their excesses far exceed his.

THE BOAT

They come very early every morning,
Young teenage girls
Neatly dressed in school uniform
Of blue skirts and white blouses.

They cram aboard the traditional African boat
That has been curved from the powerful mvule tree.
The older girls, aged about 14 years,
Pick up the oars
And position themselves at the front and back
of the boat.
The younger girls sit in the middle.
The older girls release the boat
And begin paddling away from the shore.

Singing songs in their native Rukiga language
They delve deep
Into one of the deepest lakes in Africa
Towards an island where their school is located.

None of the girls wears a life jacket.
There isn't any point
As there isn't a rescue boat available on the lake.

They arrive at the shores of the island and disembark
 Before heading off for their lessons.
The routine is repeated
In the evening as they make the return journey.

His campaign slogan is "securing your future".
During the 34 years that he has been the ruler
Nothing has changed for the girls.
They do not expect anything different.
To them, there might as well not exist a government.

THE PRINCESS

She stands upright, gazing alluringly into the camera.
Her cheerful face is pretty,
With a contagious smile.
Her hair is braided into long Swahili knots.
Her lips, luscious, and voice gentle,
She sings to the camera
"Tukutendereze Yesu" meaning
"Let us praise you Lord".

It is a traditional Christian worship song.
Her intonation is laboured and learned
With emphasis placed on the wrong consonants,
Betraying that this is not a spontaneous
Moment of worship
But a planned event.

Besides her, is a young teenage girl,
Presumably her daughter,
Who joins in the singing.

When pregnant, the princess was flown abroad
In the presidential plane,
Safe from this moribund country,
To conceive.
Perhaps this child is the fruit of that conception.

The opulent surroundings
Betray the trappings of wealth
And an upbringing of privilege.
The princess hopes to endear herself
To the impoverished youth
That can only dream of stepping onto a plane;
Their lives far detached from hers.

SECURING YOUR FUTURE

Kenya has completed their railway
From Mombasa to Kisumu.
They have opened a new rail network
From Nairobi to Nanyuki.
Their four-lane highway has been completed.
Their hospitals are our national referral hospitals.
He still promises to secure your future.

Rwanda is constructing a new international airport.
It has an orderly capital
Unlike our chaotic city
That he found organised.
He still promises to secure your future.

Tanzania has transformed its economy and
Expanded their port city.
Corruption is abhorred.
Tribalism is unknown
Yet he still promises to secure your future.

SCIENTIFIC CAMPAIGNS

They pressed for scientific campaigns
Where they hoped to dominate
The radio and television stations.
They intended to stop his message
From reaching the population.

They bought all the space
On the radio and television stations,
Switched the stations off
When he was on air.
They dragged him out of the stations,
Denying him coverage.

He turned to social media
Where he reached a wider audience.
They hacked into his online channels
But he opened other accounts.

Outsmarted, they wrote to Google and Facebook,
Urging them
To block his online accounts.
Unsuccessful,
They targeted the journalists.

Facing defeat,
They cancelled the remaining rallies
In areas where he was more popular.
They were outsmarted
In their scientific campaigns.

THE ABYSS

She is carried, shoulder high, writhing in pain,
Dazed and motionless,
Her limp shattered leg dripping with blood.
The faces of the men that carry her
Etched in horror.

This strong middle-aged woman was attending
A political rally.
The authorities began dispersing the assembly
By throwing exploding French-made tear gas canisters
At them
That are banned for use in the host country.
Shrapnel shattered her leg.

Her prognosis is not good.
She could lose her life – or her leg if she is lucky.
She is carried to a government hospital
While both health ministers remain abroad
Receiving treatment for minor ailments.

Her leg is amputated.
She is fortunate.
It could have been worse.

THE DRONE

A people-carrier vehicle
With tinted windows
That would ordinarily
Ferry passengers
From one place to another.

It is the vehicle of choice
For shadowy state officials.
It carries menacing armed men
That are up to no good.

It looks nondescript,
But when it stops
The shadowy men emerge
In front of their surprised prey,
Quickly dragging him inside.

It speeds off
To ungazetted places
With its prized cargo.
It's their mode of transport.

THE DREARY SWAMP

Metallic yellow spikes welded onto a metal ramp,
Are laid vertically across the battered tarmac road,
Blocking any traffic flow.
Uniformed officers spread out menacingly
In rows across the road.
Some are dressed in the dreaded black counter-terrorism
Police uniforms,
Others in neat white traffic police uniforms,
And more in green camouflage army fatigues.

They all wear black bullet-proof vests,
And are clad in balaclavas and helmets,
Obscuring their faces.
Automatic Kalashnikov rifles are slung across their shoulders.
Some are pressing on their triggers,
Ready to discharge ammunition
At the slightest provocation.
Expensive brand-new police vehicles and armoured
Tear gas vehicles,
Line the road behind the rows of officers.
In front of the array of officers is a rudimentary signpost
That reads "Diversion",
Even though it is a single road
With no other exit.

The dark, slim, languid man is dressed in beige khaki trousers,
A long-sleeved shirt with a sleeveless sweater on top and
Military boots.
He casually sits on top of his open roof suv
With his folded arms resting on his knees.
He is singing to the amassed soldiers,
Songs of freedom
That are blasting from a nearby vehicle.
A cameraman sits behind him,

Wearing a face mask that gives
The cameraman the appearance of a Star Wars character.

"Redemption Song" and "Murderer" are being played.
Occasionally he stands atop the vehicle
To address the soldiers
That are surrounding his convoy.
He tells them,
"You cannot kill us all" and that,
"You only die once".

The straight road cuts across a swamp that
Is in the middle of the savannah
With some tall eucalyptus trees by its side.
The temperature is hot and humid.
The sun rays are piercing down hard
On this tropical part of the pearl of Africa.
It must be very uncomfortable for everyone.

The present journalists continue to record,
And live-stream the standoff.
He has been stopped from proceeding to his next campaign rally
In the northern town of Alebtong.
The authorities have not provided any reasons for this,
Or communicated with their captive.
"Situka tutambule" meaning "Let us arise and walk",
Continues to blast out of the speakers.

A powerful country would like to sanction individuals,
Under the Magnitsky Act
Where they shall be considered,
As human rights offenders,
Be barred from entry to the country,
And have their foreign assets seized.

This encirclement is a show of defiance.
It is hollow and primitive.

SPREADING COVID-19

They claim to be stopping the spread of Covid 19
By arresting us
For not observing social distancing.
Yet, they detain us
In overcrowded cells.

Cells that do not
Observe social distancing
Where more than
Twenty of us
Are kraaled
Without being issued facemasks.

The cells are not sanitised
And detainees
Come and go.
Who is spreading Covid 19?

We are transported,
Herded like cattle
In overcrowded trucks
To overcrowded courts.

Who is spreading Covid 19?

COVID BONANZA

They locked down the country
And sought everyone's goodwill.
Companies donated vehicles and food.
Supplementary budgets were passed.
Foreign aid was received,
Yet, we were left on our own.

They ordered us to wear face masks
But did not give us any.
They told us to get tested
But charged us for the tests.
They closed the borders,
But they continued to cross them
They promised medical facilities
But turned the referral hospital
Into a VIP-only hospital.

Where did the donations go?
Who took all the money and aid?
Because we did not receive it.

The city skyline is changing
With towering new buildings
Being completed during the lock down
And expansive country homes
Being constructed.

We now know where all the donations and aid ended –
Not with us, but in their new buildings.

THE COURT MARTIAL

The dictator takes his opponents
To the court martial
To have them tried
Under military law
On concocted charges.

It is the dictator's
Weapon of choice
That he assaults
His opponents with.

Forty-eight activists
Have been charged
With possession
Of four bullets
Even though
They are civilians.

A defiant officer
That requested to retire
From the dictator's army
Was remanded
For several years
Until he apologised
To the dictator.

The court martial
Is no longer credible.
Everyone knows,
It is the dictator's weapon.

CONFLICTED POLICE

They drive recklessly,
Causing accidents,
Or hurling teargas canisters
At joyful crowds.
They strip female suspects,
Touch female suspects' breasts
And pick-pocket detainees.

Their show of bravado
Is a charade.
Deep inside
They are hurting and conflicted,
In pain from
Dire living conditions,
A diet of weevilled beans and posho,
Poor and late pay,
Embezzled SACCO funds.

They are angry,
Not because
They are nasty people
But their tormented souls
Make them misbehave.

GHETTO! CAN ANYTHING GOOD COME FROM THERE?

They did not expect anything good
To come out
Of the ghetto.
Maybe, taking drugs
And drinking cheap liquor,
They thought.

Perhaps idle youth playing
Cards and ludo.
Possibly some car mechanics
In makeshift garages
Repairing stolen vehicles,
Or Rastafarians whiling their time away.

Thieves and burglars
Reside in the ghetto,
Isn't it?
Maybe the occasional boxer
Or upcoming musician,
They believed.

He defied the labels
That society had placed on him,
Concentrated on his music
And went to school.

Until he became a parliamentarian.
That is when they took notice.
He had bigger ambitions
And went for the biggest office of the land
Leading a formidable presidential campaign.

With self- belief,
Something good came out
Of the ghetto.

ELECTIONS and COUPS

The miniscule elderly woman,
Stands in a field
Next to some shrubs.

She is dressed in a patterned kitenge
Or traditional African garb
And with a purple head dress,
Her face toughened
By the vulgarities of life.

She holds a wooden cross
While speaking to the camera.
She pleads that election-rigging
Should be treated as a coup
And that those that rig elections
Make a mockery of democracy.

She makes perfect sense
And speaks words of wisdom.
Not that the system pays attention.

Stuck in Kelsen's theories
Of the basic norm, grand norm,
And pure theory of law,
That have become an albatross
For emerging democracies.
Kelsen is used to legitimise
Illegal changes of governments.
May be, her common-sense approach
Would have better outcomes.

THE GATHERING

Their chairs are spaced
To prevent the spread of infection
At state house.
The colonial governor's residence
From where
General Tibu issues edicts and orders
Whilst superintending
Over his colony.

The former rulers
Have all resided here.
General Tibu is not an exception.
He has expanded and renovated the place
That is heavily guarded
By loyalist soldiers.

General Tibu addresses the gathered religious leaders
That have paid him homage.
Let everyone follow the law, he lectures,
And there will be peace, he adds.
It is right to have peaceful elections, he preaches,
You have no right to stop me from speaking, he gestures,
With his wide eyes darting up and down.

His opponents are besieged, as he speaks.
Barred from sleeping in hotels
Or addressing rallies.
No one pays attention to General Tibu anymore
Apart from the religious charlatans
Expecting donations
Of new vehicles
And brown envelopes
Filled with taxpayers' money.

PESTILENCE

The lakes have been taken.
The land has been appropriated.
The mines have been shared amongst themselves,
Swamps drained or
Turned into rice fields and sand mines
By the new set,
Leaving the people devoid of hope.

Education has become expensive,
Corruption legitimised,
Schools sold,
Judiciary compromised,
Parliament jettisoned,
And hospitals privatised,
Leaving the people devoid of hope.

Freedom of expression has been curtailed,
Curfews introduced,
Safe houses flourish,
Illegal detentions are ripe,
Medical ethics cast aside,
Leaving the people devoid of hope.

A pestilence has
consumed the land.
The youth are now restless and
Yearning for a new era,
When the pestilence has left the land.

THE MEANDERING BUS

It is in a dangerous mechanical condition
As it is old and done for.
Its steering wheel is bent,
the brake pads worn out,
Accelerator pedal heavy
And hand brake gone.
The shock absorbers are worn too.

It is driven by its aging driver
With poor vision,
Who refuses to brake
Or hand over to another driver.
He continues on the perilous journey
Having lost direction
And driving in a wayward way
To no particular place.

The passengers scream and shout,
Asking him to recuse himself
Or let them off
The meandering bus.
But ignoring their pleas
He locks them
Inside the bus
Where he continues to drive
Them recklessly
To nowhere.

The passengers are flying about
From left to right.
Their buttocks hurting
From the bus landing heavily
In the numerous potholes.
The aging driver
Refuses to let go of the meandering bus.

THE VOLUNTEER

In his office,
Framed pictures of the emperor
Are hanging on the painted walls.
He swears by the emperor
And his son
As he squirms his way
Around influential bloggers,
Seeking their support
For the emperor.

Bloggers that have
Received cows
As their
Pieces of silver.

To promote the emperor,
Not traditional Longhorn or Friesian cows,
But money
From the state coffers
That he,
At times, calls his.

Accused of preventing his rivals
From meeting the emperor.
He sets up his opponents,
Often ordering their arrests.
Stages dramatic encounters
To drive up ratings
Of his failing station.

His name is Balaam.
Balaam was a wicked prophet
Whose heart was not right with God.
And showed his true colours by betraying Israel.
Balaam's heart is not right with the masses.

That are vulnerable,
Due to the extreme poverty.
Vulnerable,
Due to their basic need to survive.
Vulnerable,
Due to rents owed.
Vulnerable,
Due to not affording school fees.

ORGANISING ELECTIONS or COUP?

On the day before voting
The dictator switches off
The electricity and internet,
Deploys soldiers on the streets
But claims to be organising
Free and fair elections.

He issues new guidelines
Banning congregations,
Stopping vehicles from
Accessing towns and cities,
And enforces a curfew.

He is organising a coup
And not elections.

CATFISHING

He endears himself
To the angry youth
By completing press ups,
Singing songs,
And speaking Ghetto slang.

He presents himself
As a sensitive elder
In touch with the Ghetto youth,
And appoints Ghetto youth
With names such as
"General Full Figure" and
"Butcherman" as
His presidential advisors.

Like a leopard cannot
Change its spots,
He remains a dictator,
Reliant on a loyal army
To clamp down on dissent.

He is catfishing the nation.

THE "BAYAYE"

They call them "Bayaye",
Slang for idle youth
That spend their days smoking cannabis
And committing petty crime.
Street urchins that are homeless
Having been orphaned young,
Young children
Left to sleep on the streets
And fend for themselves.

They call them "Bayaye".
Street hawkers peddling
Cheap counterfeit items.
Hustlers trying to survive
In harsh economic conditions.
Young mothers with their babies
Wrapped around their backs
Vending groundnuts.
Boxers that spend their days training.

The ministers and civil servants
That swindle government funds.
The council officials that ruthlessly
Imprison the hawkers.
The lame duck parliamentarians that
Feather their own nests
Call the downtrodden "Bayaye".

The real "Bayaye" are the officials
That have created the fake "bayaye".

THE HATCHET MAN

Bespectacled, weary, and shifty.
He is not aware of their oppression
Because
He is not on social media
And his TV subscription was
Stopped months ago.

When they are
Blocked from rallies,
He is not aware.
When the perimeter wall
Of his offices,
Is plastered with
Their demeaning pictures.
He does not notice.

He summons the opposition
For breaching guidelines
Perhaps.
He is now on social media.
He is the chairman.
Previously a prosecutor
That was sanctioned
For concocting evidence.

And elevated to a Judge
By the incumbent
From whose violations
He turns a blind eye.

THE MARKET

Bali Bakuuba is beaten and bruised.
His face is enlarged and unrecognisable.
Deformed like a hydrocephalus.
Bali Bakuuba doesn't know his assailants,
But suspects opponents of General Tibu's rule.

Bali Bakuuba was attacked in the market
By assailants shouting slogans,
And threatening to kill him.

He had gone to the market
With others,
Dressed in the council uniform.
The market is volatile,
Due to its opposition to General Tibu's rule.

"Kanyamas" or heavies

Are enforcers within the market.

The council has taken over management

From the "Kanyamas",

Who are far from pleased.

Who is benefitting

From this assault?

It is not General Tibu's opponents.

The Kanyamas are.

Bali Bakuuba's assailants.

WE ARE REMOVING A DICTATOR

"we are removing a dictator"
Is the trending hashtag.
The dictator that has stolen
Their inheritance and
Is trying to take their future.
That has impoverished their parents
And ruled them with an iron fist
For 34 years.

"We are removing a dictator"
That has desecrated their land,
That is an absolute dictator
That imprisons and kills
With impunity.

"We are removing a dictator"
That revels in threatening
To crush and kill them.
That locks them up
In safe houses
Where they are tortured.
A dictator that
Galivants about
Like a medieval king.

"We are removing a dictator"
That has taken control
Of the nation's coffers.
That bribes opportunists
With taxpayers' funds.
That calls the oil reserves "his oil".
That behaves like Mansa Musa
By dishing out state funds
At his whims.

The subjects are exhausted
And broken.
They no longer simply look on.
After all,
They have nothing to lose.
Their options are bleak.
That is why,
They have chosen
"To remove a dictator".

THE FART

The emperor is standing by a microphone,
Addressing his minions.
They are sitting under a large tent dressed in
Yellow shirts.
He is bald, having shaved off all his hair,
And wearing a yellow long-sleeved shirt.
Yellow is the colour of choice of his ruling party.

Speaking his local dialect he tells the gathered audience
in Runyankole, that "a friendship pact based on
Loose sexual encounters is ruined by a fart".
The audience laugh uncomfortably.

"If your friend farts, why should that
Ruin your friendship?" he ponders.
"If your friendship was strong, the fart
Should not have ruined your friendship," he cautions.

Corruption and nepotism have been the hallmark
Of his long rule.
He has farted on his subjects for a long time.
The pact with his subjects was broken
A long time ago.

THE FLAG

Though a heavy boot lands on his back,
He still holds onto it.
Even though a heavy blow strikes his rib cage,
He still does not let go.
When violently dragged on the tarmac,
He still holds onto it.

The black, yellow, and red flag
Is firmly held in his palms.
Black for his blackness,
Yellow for the ever-present sun,
And red for the blood that unites us all.

With a crested crane in the middle
Signifying the natural beauty
Of the country.
The flag is swaying and slaying
Like a model on the catwalk.

Though outnumbered
He is not shaken.
Beaten and bruised,
He remains firm in his convictions.
Abused,
He remains defiant.
The flag shall rise again.

OOMPA LOOMPA MINISTER

The Oompa Loompa urges him
To continue singing and dancing.
That he did not fight
For a musician to become president.

The Oompa Loompa did not resign
When he was accused of corruption,
Or when he has been
Involved in dalliances
With underage girls.

The potbellied Oompa Loompa
Has questionable academic certificates,
But is still
A senior official.

On whose behalf does Oompa Loompa minister speak?
Today's youth were
Not yet born
When he was fighting
In the bushes
That have since been cut down
By greedy officials.

THE NEW CONSTITUTION

It was celebrated
As the dawn of a new era,
Where the rule of law prevailed.
Presidential term limits and
Age limit provisions
Were entrenched.

To avoid a return
To the previous era
They claimed was lawless,
And that the rulers
Changed the constitution
Whimsically.

Until the emperor
Wanted to rule forever
And yet
The provisions in the new constitution
Hindered him.

That is when
He touched it,
Changed it,
Like a roll of toilet paper,
Rendering it worthless
And powerless
From stopping him
From ruling forever.

ODE to MUKWANO

He was a prosperous and industrious
Ugandan of Asian origin
That employed many,
Including myself,
After I completed my university studies.

Still young, naïve, and restless,
I was ushered into his office
Where, after a brief chit chat,
He asked,
How much do you want to be paid?
I answered with a salary figure.
He did not haggle and agreed.
His word was his bond.

I was later transferred to Fort Portal
Where he owned tea factories.
We travelled in his Mercedes cross country
And talked the whole journey.
It was my first time in that part of the country.

He was fatherly and unassuming,
Yet one of the wealthiest individuals.
He advised to be wary of others
Within the company.
He provided accommodation
And ensured that everyone's
Salary was promptly paid
Every month.

At the factories,
He ate his lunch
In the staff canteen
With the other employees
That he treated like his family.

He was a humble
And down to earth person
That valued all.
They called him "Mukwano",
Meaning "friendship".

Amirali Karmali died on 10 July.

DISASSOCIATIVE EPISODES

He calls himself
A pan-Africanist,
But metes out
Violence to Africans.
He calls himself
A freedom fighter
But doesn't tolerate dissent.

He says he wants a united continent,
But disunites it
By engaging in wars
In neighbouring states.

He calls himself a democrat,
But stifles democracy.
He says, "Africa's problem
Is leaders that overstay".
And yet he has ruled
For thirty-four years.

He has disassociative episodes.

SMALL TALK

Approaching the outskirts of Nateete,
A bustling centre outside the capital city,
A female traffic police officer
Dressed in crisp white uniform
Flags the vehicle down.

Like the driver,
She is an Atesot
From the east of the country.
It's a random stop
As the driver has not made any violations.

She engages in small talk,
Asking where we are coming from.
She then remarks,
"You have been visiting your relatives?"
Displaying her home sickness.

She switches to her native Itesot language
And engages with the driver in small talk
Whilst musing in English
About how she misses Soroti.

It is getting late.
The driver offers her
Some money
Before she lets us go.
Leaving here is not for the fainthearted.

TEAR DROPS

My spirit is weary.
I once walked with my head held high
But now,
Rejection and frustration are the norm.
Oppression and repression thrive.
My hopes have been shattered.

We worked hard for ourselves
But now have to beg you.
The humiliation breaks me.
I left my country because of you.

When you see me bitter,
Do not be surprised.
I left my country because of you.

I could have been anything,
But you took away all the opportunities.
You stole my future, even my certificates.
Your rendered them worthless
By employing your relatives.

I now wait on my Redeemer to save me
And yet I know that he also is tortured.

You own all the malls and arcades,
Leaving others hopeless.
I have lost hope.
Betrayal aches.
I left the country because of you.

My pain is calmed
By the hope that I have.
My spirit soothed by my Saviour.
I know that my hope is near.

I know what to do,
Everyone knows what to do.

At the ballot box,
I beseech you
To remain firm so that
We can be joyful in the new era
Where there is no tear gas,
Where there are no curfews,
Where he does not threaten
To crush us.
Where we are all equal.

A new era, without safe houses,
Without four-wheel drives with sirens
Shoving us off the roads.
Where the hospitals have medication
And we all walk majestically
Because we are proud of our country.

I beseech everyone from near and far
That what we have always longed for
Is on the horizon.

I mourn for my country.
We all know what to do
At the ballot box
So that
We are not enslaved again.

POETIC JUSTICE

"They have not written"
Even to say,
"We are going to switch you off",
Laments the mouthpiece
That would like equity.
And yet his hands are stained.

His government switched
The internet off
Without warning.
They levy a charge
On social media use
And hack into online pages.

The tables have turned
And their social media pages
Have been taken down.
They have thrived on
Impunity far too long.

Poetic justice exists!

A PYRRHIC VICTORY
Election, January 2021

After announcing the results
Of the rigged elections
And declaring victory,
The cities and towns
Are surrounded
By military tanks and soldiers.

Opposition polling agents
Are abducted and detained,
Their declaration forms
Confiscated.

The soldiers that surround
The cities and towns
Were recruited
From the same people
That they are
Expected to brutalise.

The watchman stands
Guard in vain.
The soldiers suffer
The same if not
Worse injustices
Than the people.

Their heist has been
Too obvious this time.

This is a pyrrhic victory.

Printed by: Copytech (UK) Limited trading as
Printondemand-worldwide.com
9 Culley Court, Bakewell Road, Orton Southgate,
Peterborough, PE2 6XD